Maria Publig

MOZART

BONECHI VERLAG STYRIA

CONTENTS

Vertrieb
für Österreich
VERLAG STYRIA
Schönaugasse 64
A-8010 GRAZ

für Deutschland
AZN
Hooge Weg 71
D-47623 Kevelaer

für die Schweiz
Herder AG Basel
Muttenzerstraße 109
CH-4133 Pratteln 1

MOZART
Publication created and designed by: Casa Editrice Bonechi
Publication Manager: Monica Bonechi
Graphic design and Layout: Sonia Gottardo
Cover and Make-up: Alberto Douglas Scotti
Editing: Anna Baldini

Text: Maria Publig
Translation: Traduco Snc, Florence

© Copyright by Casa Editrice Bonechi
via Cairoli 18/b I-50131 - Florence
E-mail: bonechi@bonechi.it - Internet: www.bonechi.it

Printed in Italy by Centro Stampa Editoriale Bonechi

PHOTOGRAPHIC REFERENCES

Photographs from archives of Casa Editrice Bonechi taken by Marco Banti, Gianni Dagli Orti, Luigi Di Giovine, Paolo Giambone, Andrea Pistolesi, *except:*

Historisches Museum der Stadt Wien: p. 4 (*below*), 6 (*below*), 7, 8 (*below*), 9 (*above*), 10 (*below right*), 19, 30 (*below*), 32, 33 (*above*), 34 (*below right*), 35, 40 (*above*), 41, 42 (*above and below left*), 45, 47 (*below*), 54 (*above*), 55 (*below*), 56, 57, 58, 59 (*above*), 60 (*above left*), 62. – Internationale Stiftung Mozarteum, Salzburg: p. 10 (*above*), 11, 21, 22 (*below*), 26 (*below*), 27 (*above*), 33 (*below right*), 34 (*above and below left*), 43 (*below*), 52 (*above*), 61. – Wiener Stadt- und Landesbibliothek: p. 10 (*below left*), 42 (*below right*), 48 (*above*), 52 (*below*), 53 (*right*). – Österreichische Nationalbibliothek, Vienna: p. 14, 18, 30 (*above*), 43 (*above*). – Kunsthistorisches Museum, Vienna: p. 3, 4 (*above*), 5, 51. – Haus-, Hof- und Staatsarchiv, Vienna (Fotostudio Otto, Vienna): p. 33 (*below left*). – Sammlungen der Gesellschaft der Musikfreunde in Wien: Cover illustration, p. 46. – Graphische Sammlung Albertina, Vienna: p. 49 (*above*). – Museum Carolino Augusteum, Salzburg: p. 12 (*right*). – Erzbischöfliches Dom- und Diözesanmuseum, Vienna: p. 59 (*below*). – Dommuseum Salzburg: p. 22 (*above*). – Stift Herzogenburg: p. 60 (*above right*). – Private collection: p. 55 (*above*). – Schwarzenbergische Archive, Schloß Murau: p. 50. – Goethe-Museum, Düsseldorf: p. 60 (*below*). – Historisches Museum Frankfurt am Main: p. 49 (*below*). – Hunterian Art Gallery, University of Glasgow: p. 38. – Columbia University, New York: p. 44. – Muzeum Hlavniho Mesta Prahy: p. 48 (*below*). – Archiv der Salzburger Festspiele: p. 54 (*below*). – Photo of the Vatican Museums: p. 24, 25. – Civico Museo Bibliografico Musicale, Comune di Bologna: p. 26 (*above*). – Raccolta delle Stampe Achille Bertarelli - Castello Sforzesco (Comune di Milano: Direzione Civiche Raccolte d'arte applicata ed incisioni): p. 23.

Cover: Barbara Krafft (1764-1825), Wolfgang Amadeus Mozart, Oil on canvas (1819).

ISBN 3-222-12513-9

* * *

INTRODUCTION

Wolfgang Amadeus Mozart's infancy spanned the close of the splendid baroque period represented in all its exuberance by the Empress Maria Theresa. Festivities were celebrated and the Empress, then still young, performed before audiences in the works of her maestro Metastasio and dedicated her entire energy to the education of her sixteen children and the careful management of state affairs.

In the meantime her spouse Francis Stephen of Lorraine often got bored and entertained himself with attractive dames which plunged the Empress into deep distress. She was as wilful in guiding the Austrian State and the military conflicts with the King of Prussia Federick II, as she was submissive in her private life: she always forgave her husband. He had carte blanche for whatever he wanted to do, even for example being initiated into the then emerging Masonry, an association that from 1717 had spread from England throughout the whole of Europe.

The ideas of the Enlightenment were important for passing from a purely theocratic worldview, still popular at the beginning of the baroque period, to one which on the other hand pivoted around the earth.

Masonry contributed to the rapid diffusion of scientific notions and the curtailing of the absolute power of the Church on state affairs and on the Emperor (Empress).

Man's task on earth was not only, according to the outlook of the Church, to prepare himself for life after death, but rather to achieve for his fellows and for himself an existence as worthy as possible of being led.

It was thus more than revolutionary not only that Maria Theresa should have reforms drafted by declared masons such as Joseph von Sonnenfels and Gottfried van Swieten and that she should heed their advice, but that even her spouse Emperor Francis should adhere to that association.

As for herself, she was very sceptical about Masonry, above all because, as a woman, she would have been barred from initiation. She nevertheless tolerated sympathy for the Enlightened reformers, sympathy also felt by her eldest son, Joseph, who however never belonged to the association; his love for freedom had not made him break away from the Church only to land up in another dependency.

On the contrary, with the *Edict on Masonry* which he published in 1785, he reduced the uncontrollable abuses of the various esoteric associations like those of the Rosicrucians, the Illuminati and many others, including Freemasons.

By means of this edict the secret activity of the lodges was severely forbidden and the number of actually operating ones was reduced. In 1765 the Empress Maria Theresa appointed her son Joseph co-regent conferring on him the task of introducing and carrying out reforms in the military system. He was also ap-

Canaletto: Vienna seen from the Belvedere, 1759/60.

pointed Grand Master of all the knightly orders.

The edicts for the abolition of torture (1776) and of serfdom, also date back to the period of his mother's reign, as does the introduction of compulsory elementary education, that was to be the first stage towards equal opportunity also for

Canaletto: The Freyung in Vienna, 1758/61. In his first journey to Vienna, at the age of six, Mozart also performed in Countess Maria Theresia Kinsky's house, located in Herrengasse, near the Freyung.

The Empress Maria Teresa, together with her spouse, Francis of Lorraine, and most of her children in a copy of a work by Martin van Meytens, painted by Johann Gottfried Haid in 1756, year in which Mozart was born.

Maria Teresa succeeded to the throne at the age of twenty-three. She governed Austria for 40 years. Painting by Martin van Meytens.

the lower social classes, still a very distant goal.

In 1780, after a forty-year rule, Maria Theresa died and was succeeded by her firstborn, Emperor Joseph II. The new sovereign hastened to bring about all the transformations concerning ideas and reforms, that had not been carried out while his mother was still alive. He himself had already done much to foster change in the government system. Now what he was facing, for the first time, was a huge obstacle: to repress the excessive interference of the Roman Church in Austria's social life.

The Empress Maria Theresa had been a profoundly pious woman. Joseph had often had the occasion of observing how the clergy managed to convince Maria Theresa to give them concessions. Thus, under her rule, church reforms could not have been conceivable.

The bigotry of a part of the Roman Church had seemed overpowering even to the both Enlightened and religious Mozart family. Leopold, Wolfgang's father, who at first had thought of becoming a parish priest, described certain ecclesiastics as 'Schrollen' (eccentric). Wolfgang himself made fun, by shaking his head, of the immoral attitude of certain monks. This is what he wrote from Italy: 'we have had the honour of exchanging visits with a certain Dominican who passes for a saint, but I do not really think so at all, seeing that for breakfast he often takes a cup of chocolate and thereupon a hearty glass of strong Spanish wine. I have also had the honour

The 'Am Hof' church in the homonymous square. At no. 13, in the house of Count Collalto, Nannerl and Wolfgang performed for the first time in Vienna, on 9 October, 1762, in a private concert.

In 1782, Pope Pius VI arrived in Vienna with his entourage for negotiations with the Emperor Joseph II. From the balcony of the 'Am Hof' church, he gave the Easter blessing. Coloured copper-plate engraving, by Carl Schütz.

The Emperor Joseph II governed for 10 years together with his mother Maria Teresa, succeeding her as sole regent on her death in 1780. Oil painting by Joseph Hickel, 1771.

of dining with this saint, that at table drank his wine, like a good sport, and, to finish his meal had a glass full of strong wine, two good slices of melon, peaches, pears, five cups of coffee, an entire plate full of game birds, two servings of milk with lemon.'

To pass reforms the consent of a large part of the population was ready to be had. Joseph II exploited this favourable moment, abolishing 700 monasteries within the space of eight days. He also reduced the number of regular religious from 63,000 to 27,000. He placed the oldest male and female monastic orders under the control of the bishop.

He himself wanted to acquire more information on the general trend of the Church and exercise a greater influence on it. To avoid the worst, in 1782 Pope Pius IV in person arrived in Vienna. Joseph II aimed for an independent Austrian State Church. The confiscated patrimony of the abolished monasteries was administered through a religious fund used for the livelihood of parish priests and other needs. The Church had to be at the service of others and not vice versa. In 1781 the Emperor Joseph II passed the Patent of Tolerance that from that moment onwards guaranteed freedom of creed to Protestants, Jews and the followers of other doctrines. Like his mother before him, Joseph II dedicated himself with great zeal to the promotion of hospitals, orphanages, alms-houses and institutions for the poor be-

Today, in the Hofburg, winter residence of the Austrian Emperor, there is part of the National Austrian Library. The equestrian statue of the Emperor Joseph II adorns the entrance opening onto Josephplatz.

The Hofbibliothek. Coloured copper-plate engraving by Carl Shütz, 1780.

sides the training of a sufficient number of doctors and other hospital staff. In support of the new regulation of the relation between the State and the Church, Joseph II opted for the definite abolition of the death penalty (1787).

Notwithstanding, he was himself forced, before dying (on 20 February 1790), to revoke many of his reforms. After all, the people felt overwhelmed by his numerous innovations. Even his political defeat in numerous warfares, contributed to undermining the monarch's authority. With more rigorous firmness Joseph's younger brother, Leopold of Tuscany, intervened from 1790, as the new Emperor. Many of the progressive ideals, object of public debate, were newly suffocated under his rule. Nevertheless, the emancipation of the middle class, once introduced, did not allow itself to be suppressed. These social classes had been too deeply imbued with Enlightened ideas of equal dignity for all men. Having sufficient financial means, assisted by a good, solid upbringing and university education, it was possible, even in the Eighteenth Century to improve to a considerable degree one's personal, professional, and social standing.

The Mozarts made use of this newly-acquired, middle-class consciousness in all their encounters with the nobility. In this way they proved themselves to be the true pioneers of a liberal society, even though it was still a long way off.

Mozart was happy to take long walks with his wife Constanze in the Prater. The 'Lusthaus' (brothel) was built in 1781, year in which Mozart moved to Vienna. Coloured etching by Johann Ziegler, 1783.

The monument of Maria Teresa is situated between the two finest museums in Vienna: the Kunsthistorisches and the Naturhistorisches Museum. Famous personalities among whom Gluck, Mozart, and Haydn, are commemorated in the high-reliefs of the gables.

INFANCY AND BOYHOOD

When Wolfgang Amadeus Mozart arrived with his family for the first time in Vienna, he had already had many experiences. Differently from his six-year-old peers, he always found himself in the limelight in no matter what society. Wherever he went music lovers and curious on-lookers hastened in crowds, fascinat-ed, then would go about publicizing the performance of the child prodigy that they had attended. The child, born on 27 January 1756, was natu-rally aware of having extraordinary musical talents. Already in Salzburg, his birthplace, he had been the object

of particular admiration. With his sister Maria Anna nicknamed Nan-nerl he attended with unerring inter-est his father's sessions of chamber music. Leopold a native of Augs-burg, was a violinist and 'Hof-und-Kammer-componist'(chamber-musi-cian and Court-composer) to the Court Chapel of the Archbishop of Salzburg Sigismund Schrattenbach, and from 1763 Vice-Kapellmeister.
It was chiefly the friends of the Mozart family who recorded the var-ious episodes of young Wolfgang's infancy. Anton Schachtner for exam-ple, regarding the five-year-old child's constant insistence on play-ing with others, thus recalls; 'Wolf-gang was playing the violin with me, I noticed to my great surprise that I was totally superfluous there, I laid aside my violin in silence and looked at (his) Father whose cheeks at this sight were streaked with tears of ad-miration and comfort'.
His mother Anna Maria observed everything with a certain benevolent detachment, throwing in a remark from time to time and always main-taining her good humour. The at-mosphere in the Mozart family was simple and serene, the relation be-tween its members was full of deep affection and humanity. When music was played the children dedicated

Mozart's father, Leopold Mozart, with his children. Copper-plate engraving by Jean Baptiste Delafosse, 1764.

"Bastienne", French comic opéra. Frontispiece, 1764.

After his reception in Schönbrunn, Mozart received the gala outfit of the little Archduke, Maximillian as a present. In an engraving of 1764, Pietro Antonio Lorenzoni ensured for posterity an image of the proud musician at the age of six.

Mozart's mother, Anna Maria Walpurga Mozart, née Pertl.
Oil painting by Rosa Hagenauer-Barducci, 1775 circa.

Mozart's father, Leopold Mozart. Oil painting, presumably
by Pietro Antonio Lorenzoni, 1765 circa.

We owe to Leopold Mozart the standard teaching method
for violin still used today: 'Versuch einer gründlichen
violinschule' (1756). Frontispiece.

themselves to study with great pleasure. Their father
Leopold was at the same time the children's teacher.
He had been almost predestined to this task by his teaching the choirboys in Salzburg. Thus he was also perfectly
aware of how much he could expect out of children. Nannerl and the young Wolfgang learnt everything through
play and for that purpose they were allowed almost
everything. 'When he learnt to count, the table, the
chairs, the walls, and even the floor were covered with
figures', noted Schachtner. In that period, they also set
out willingly on walks and excursions. The destination of
these outings was unfailingly Maria Plain, Hellbrunn,

Hallein, but also included St Gilgen, his mother's birthplace, where she had spent 27 years living in the Law Courts. This was also the establishment and workshop of Nannerl's future husband, Baron Berchthold of Sonnenburg, he too like Nannerl's grandfather, a prefect.

While Wolfgang as an adult moved to Vienna, Nannerl remained in Salzburg territory. Later, following her husband's death, she returned to Salzburg and lived next door to the woman that other than herself Mozart loved best; his wife Constanze.

The Mozart family lived in their home at 9 Getreidegasse up to 1773. They later moved into the 'Tanzmeisterhaus', in the Hannibalplatz (today 8 Makartplatz).

An ancient view of the house in which Wolfgang Amadeus Mozart was born. The Mozarts lived on the third floor.

Today one can still see (and sometimes even listen to) one of Mozart's pianos.

In the Autumn of 1762, the family went for the first time to Vienna. Before having paid the compulsory toll at the gate of the town, they stopped in Passau - among other reasons also to not tire the children. The canon of that place, Count Herberstein, a benevolent patron of the Mozarts', did not hesitate to personally accompany the family to Linz to announce their arrival. He thereupon declared himself ready to escort them, as their patron, up to Vienna 'and he will cause a great stir there, ahead of them'. In Ybbs on the Danube, Wolfgang performed a rapid demonstration on the organ, to then conquer by storm the Viennese society. The two children were always about, footloose, making trouble. Hence sometimes even their parents, in whose opinion the children were 'amusing, but also mischievous', complained. Like wild, little characters they also attended the concert held in Schönbrunn at the Empress Maria Theresa's palace on 13 October 1762, from 3 to 6 in the afternoon. After Mozart's performance 'he flew into the Empress's lap, he embraced her and kissed her roundly'. And thereupon the little man proposed to the darling princess Marie Antoinette (who was later beheaded in France). From then on, the Mozart family was on everyone's mouth. They returned to Salzburg with their pockets well replenished.

Nannerl and Wolfgang confidently performed their concert before the Imperial family.

No Mozart fan and no visitor to Vienna ever forgets to admire in this town the hall of Schönbrunn where Mozart celebrated his first great success.

A monument opposite the town house of St Gilgen reminds us that Mozart came from, on his mother's side, this locality of Salzkammergut.
Today, in the building that was once the seat of the Law Courts and later the residence of Mozart's sister, Nannerl, is a small, charming Mozartian museum.

View of St Gilgen and of the Wolfgangsee.

The picturesque surroundings of the castle of Helbrunn were the welcome destination of the outings of the Mozart family.

For a long time Mozartian research studies supposed that the coronation mass in C Major (K 317) was dedicated to the miraculous image in the Wallfahrtkirche by Maria Plain.

TRAVELS AND INTERNATIONAL CONTACTS

Since the journey to Vienna had been undertaken with such success, a grand, minutely planned itinerary could not but be decided on there and then. That circumstance, according to a rather superficial view, was to later earn Leopold Mozart the reputation of having behaved like a greedy and selfish person. This reproach must be reconsidered if one is only to think that up until the last century heavy child labour was taken for granted worldwide. After all, only in 1987 did the UN guarantee the rights of children. Our opinion and our moral judgement concerning a situation of that time must then be placed in a different perspective that keeps in mind the span of two hundred and twenty-five years. His family was resolved on a grand European tour that in those days was comparable to a world tour. The children led in the meantime their normal everyday life. Obviously work and play were reconciled in a leisurely manner even during the journey. They travelled in a private luxury coach; the money necessary for the trip had been borrowed from the Hagenauer family, friends of theirs, who ran a grocer's shop (a shop with many gourmet specialities) in the house where Mozart was born, at 9 Getreidegasse. In 1763 they started off happily on their long tour of Europe.

Over a more than three year period, the Mozarts visited almost all the most important cities in Germany among which Monaco, Augsburg, Ulm, Ludwisburg, Schwetzingen, Heidelberg, Mainz, Frankfurt, Koblenz, Bonn, Cologne and Aachen.

In Belgium, for the first time, young Mozart could not understand a thing because there 'they do not speak a word of German, but pure Walloon, that is bad French'.

In Brussels they remained overwhelmed by the abundance of art treasures. Guided by original works, the children were introduced to the international history of art. Leopold thus summed up: 'Here one can see in every church a great quantity of works of the most famous artists. Night and day, I have before my eyes a painting of Rubens, housed in the main church, which depicts Christ handing the keys to Peter before the other Apostles. The figures are life-size'.

The charm and importance of this journey certainly did not reside uniquely in its financial aspect. 'Travel (which) broadens the mind' and the observation of other regions and other people linked with travelling were later on to reveal themselves to be fundamental also for Mozart's general culture. For the Enlightened Leopold Mozart, so full of interests, it was natural to broaden one's horizon and transform the impressions gained into creative impulses.

Notwithstanding all statements to the contrary, during its journey the well-to-do Mozart family had, for the first time, come to a certain extent into contact with the poverty in large towns.

At Versailles, for example, there was a particularly violent contrast between the financially remunerative pomp and performances at King Louis XV's palace and at the houses of the entire nobility and the sad,

Viennese street scene opposite the Augustinerkirche. Drawing by Salomon Kleiner. Viennese traffic in those days was as hazardous as that of modern times!

This portrait of Mozart's brother as a young man was commissioned by Nannerl after his death. Gouache on parchment, 1803.

The castle of Versailles in a painting by Pierre-Denis Martin of 1772. Mozart refused the post as organist that he had been offered here.

King Louis XV by Pierre-Adrien Gois (1731-1823).

miserable street life. The appalled Leopold related in his letters to Salzburg: 'He will not easily find a place with such a lot of poor and mutilated people. After having spent only a minute in church and having crossed just a few streets he is approached by a blind man, a cripple, a lame man, a beggar in a state of near putrifaction, or else sees someone lying on the street whose hand was devoured in childhood by a pig.

The *Sonatas for Violin and Piano* (K 6, 7, 8 and 9) of young Wolfgang were sent to be printed by Leopold; a very costly affair in those days.

Naturally also in Paris Mozart gained a wide knowledge of the composing style in fashion in that country. However he set his joyous expectations on London. There Bach's youngest son, Johann Christian, performed in all of Europe, revolutionizing the musical scene of the epoch with new expressive forms, in particular the *Allegro cantante*, forerunners of classicism.

The seven-year-old Mozart emulated Johann Christian Bach's lively sonorous language in his *Symphony in E Flat Major* (K 16) created while he was waiting to be able to perform before King George III and his spouse Charlotte. Even so, the Mozarts remained greatly surprised by the couple's bearing, since 'the social relations of both and their friendly ways would never have made us suppose them to be the King and Queen of England'.

The famous castrato Giovanni Manzuoli who was then performing in London, befriended the child prodigy; thus the Mozarts, imbued with new impressions, began after two years and a half the return journey home, passing through Holland, once more through Brussels and Paris and finally crossing Switzerland and Germany, to Salzburg.

THE PERIOD
OF STUDY
AND CREATION

The Mozarts did not remain for long in Salzburg. They rested, elaborated the impressions received during their long journey. Wolfgang began to dedicate himself in a systematic way to the study of composition. The expert pedagogue Leopold chose the levels of difficulty with insight and encouraged, in a differentiated way, the capacities of his son and his daughter. In fact, even Nannerl composed and played the piano in an excellent manner. Nevertheless in 1769 when Wolfgang went with his father on his first grand tour to Italy, she remained at home. The Enlightened Leopold had already dared too much, for those days, in giving his daughter an education almost equal to that of Wolfgang. On the other hand the girl's ability and intellectual faculties could be considered an obstacle by potential Salzburg husbands. Her accomplishments did not conform with the current scale of feminine values. She married only at thirty-three years of age, with a man fifteen years her elder, twice widowed and fitted out with five children.

Wolgang had to pursue his travels in any case. A musician who wanted to obtain good job opportunities for the future, had to begin in time to build himself a splendid reputation in Italy. Hence, in the Autumn of 1769, the Mozarts went to Rovereto, the first stop of the grand tour planned for Italy. And already here Mozart was acclaimed as a star: 'Even though only 6 or 8 personalities had been informed of our arrival here; we found all of Rovereto gathered in church and strong young men had to precede us to clear the way up to the choir where we struggled for almost a quarter of an hour to reach the organ, because everyone wanted to be the nearest'.

Artistic appreciation did not surely have first place in the interests of the people. The sensationalism of events created much more enthusiasm. In addition to his excellent musical training, Mozart had learnt not to disregard even a certain stagy effect. He played blindfolded, with

Maria Anna (Nannerl) von Berchtold zu Sonnenburg.
Oil painting of 1785 ca.

The Baron Johann Baptist von Berchtold zu Sonnenburg.
Oil painting of 1785 ca.

The Archbishop Hieronymus, Count Colloredo didn't make life easy for Mozart in Salzburg. Oil painting by Franz Xaver König, around 1773.

One of the most famous portraits of the musician in that it is among the most faithful: the Mozart family (Mozart's mother, already deceased, is depicted in the medallion), by Johann Nepomuk della Croce, 1780/81.

two fingers and he always made use of new sensational effects. Hence he took for granted the audience's enthusiasm.

They later continued to Milan and Verona where they naturally attended the lyrical theatre learning of new operas.

The Veronese nobility was a fine art connoisseur. Mozart's admission to the famous *Accademia Filarmonica* and his appointment as honorary maestro to its Chapel was inevitable. In Bologna, the stronghold of intellectuals, their contact with Marshal Giovanni Luca Pallavicini was fundamental. However, besides submitting all the indispensable testimonials, the Mozarts concentrated themselves on one man only: Padre Giovanni Battista Martini. The latter was the grey eminence of the international musical scene. Those who were equal to his requests, had access to the entire high society.

Although he had very difficult tastes, he accepted the task of preparing the fourteen-year-old Wolfgang to sit for the extremely tough admission examination to the *Accademia Filarmonica* of Bologna that Mozart, despite the messages of rejoicing of Leopold to Salzburg, managed to pass only with great difficulty and with the furtive help of

Padre Martini during the written test. The following stops were Florence and Rome whose magnificence and lavish lifestyle greatly struck the Mozarts. Here too Wolfgang did his best to cause a sensation. Hence in the Sistine Chapel he wrote out from memory, certainly without errors, Gregorio Allegri's *Miserere* even though the pope had 'forbidden on pain of excommunication' its transcription.

Nevertheless Pope Clemence XIV appointed him *Knight of the Golden Spur* authorizing him in this way to boast of the title of *Cavaliere*.

Even in Naples Mozart attended the theatre to gain inspiration for the opera he had been commissioned to write in Milan and for the production of which he returned to that city on 18 October 1770. He had already composed a part of the recitative for the opera seria *Mitridate, re di Ponto* (K 74a/87) in Salzburg. The arias on the other hand were normally created on the spot, tailor-maded for the singers, both female and male, and for the musicians.

Alongside the tiring work of composition and production, in that period the Mozarts had, as often occurred, to deal with numerous intricate situations.

Mozart had already prepared a fair

amount of material for the second opera that he had been commissioned in Milan. Both this opera, *Ascanio in Alba* (K 111) (1771) and the third opera for Milan, *Lucio Silla* (K 135) (1772) were much applauded.

Five years later, in 1777, the urge to act newly attracted Mozart to faraway places. There followed once again a grand German tour that had Paris as its final destination. Mozart's father, by order of the new Prince-Archbishop Yeronimus Colloredo, had to remain in Salzburg. His place was taken by Mozart's mother Anna Maria who, however,

CAV. AMADEO WOLFGANGO MOZART ACCAD. FILARMON: DI BOLOG.
E DI VERONA

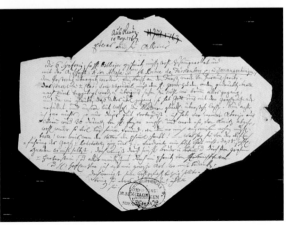

Mozart portrayed as 'Knight of the Golden Spur'.
Oil painting, 1777.

Letter of Leopold Mozart, written from Olmütz, on
10 November, 1767 to Lorenz Hagenauer, landlord of his
house in Salzburg.

was never again to see her city since, on 3 July 1778, she died in solitude in Paris. Wolfgang had kept her very little company.

Before arriving in Paris, in Mannheim, she had found herself fighting a losing battle when she had tried to persuade her obstinate son against his great unrequited love for Aloysia Weber. Actually they had stopped there so that Wolfgang could attend the famous school in Mannheim in which pioneer expressive means regarding composition and instrumentation indicated to young composers the future trends of the musical art. His friendship with the Weber family absorbed however so much time that in Salzburg Leopold almost lost his patience.

The twenty-one year old Wolfgang had, formerly, already fallen for women and especially (in Augsburg) for his cousin Maria Anna Thekla, nicknamed Bäsle. At the end of his return trip from Paris she accompanied her cousin Wolfgang to Salzburg to comfort him and the rest of his deeply grieved family for their irreparable loss.

The journey, all in all, even not considering this great, unpredictable

sorrow, had not been at all a success. In the end it only produced expenses, not repaid by commissions for compositions. The only real opportunity, a position of organist at the court of Versailles, was refused by Mozart in the grips of an untimely pride. He wanted to avoid a bureaucratic musical career.

St Eustache's Church in Paris. Engraving of the eighteenth century.

Mozart's mother died at the age of 57, on 3 July 1778, during a journey to Paris and was buried the following day in the cemetery of St Eustache's.

THE ROUTINE OF DAILY LIFE IN SALZBURG

The period passed by Mozart in Salzburg was notthe happiest of his life. It often occurs that, for the most part, prophets are not recognized in their own country. Those who have followed from close up the development of a man cannot judge with detachment his maturity and his worth, even though the whole of Salzburg was naturally astonished by Wolfgang's talent.

At the age of five, Wolfgang had already celebrated his theatrical debut with *Sigismundus* by Johann Ernst Eberlin and composed his first pieces. At the age of thirteen he was appointed *(unpaid) third Konzert-meister (concert-master)* of the Hofkapelle of Salzburg. The then Archbishop Sigismundus Schrattenbach did not pose an obstacle to the needs of the Mozarts to perfect their art. He allowed them to travel whenever and wherever they wished. Concerning this matter he exempted Leopold from service.

It was thus much more painful when, after his death, the prosaic Illuminist, Hieronymus Colloredo, succeeded him in office. At first everything seemed to go as usual. Mozart was promoted to the paid post of Konzertmeister. The dramatic serenade *Il sogno di Scipione* (K 126), homage to the Prince, originally conceived for Schrattenbach, was now retailored for Colloredo.

Mozart, then in his early adolescence, made continuous demands and spoke of his master using numerous impertinences. These circumstance referred to Hieronymus certainly did not favour his benevolence towards Mozart.

Just before their journey to Paris, Leopold and Wolfgang were dismissed from service (1777) because the Archbishop demanded the presence of his musicians. While his father managed to have himself taken on again, the son wanted to try his luck elsewhere, convinced that, in any other place he would be more welcome than in his native city, which he turned his back on forever four years later, in March 1781. In 1779, thanks to Leopold's obsequious pleas, he was readmitted to Colloredo's service. Several musicians, who had been living in the city for some time, considered Mozart a failure since he had returned to Salzburg after his journey

The monument of Mozart in the Mozartplatz in Salzburg. The project and the model of the work are by the sculptor Monaco Ludwig Schwanthaler.

to Paris. Their cynical remarks further damaged his relation with Colloredo. The commission for the opera seria *Idomeneo, re di Creta* (K 366) was for Wolfgang Mozart (he signed his works Amadé or Amadeo; posterity was to call him Wolfgang Amadeus Mozart) the favourable occasion to escape, once again, from Salzburg.

The Elector Karl Theodor had commissioned him to compose the opera on recommendation of old friends from Munich: Christian Cannabich, Friedriech Raum, and Anton Raaff. The libretto was written by the Salzburg Abbé Giambattista Varesco who tackled the text in a somewhat clumsy manner. For the first time Mozart imposed the rigour of his dramatic spirit. He began making changes, on his own initiative, sometimes putting Varesco before the fait accompli.

The Greek Idomeneo has promised the Gods, in thanksgiving for his return home to his homeland after the war, to sacrifice the first person he encounters. This happens to be his son Idamante. The dramatic and spiritual conflicts between the promise made and his love for his son are finally solved to the general satisfaction of all. The Elector had already attended, with enthusiasm, the rehearsals. On 26 January, 1781, Leopold and Nannerl left for Munich to attend the performance and the Carnival.

Hieronymus Colloredo was engaged on a visit to Vienna with his entire entourage. Only the Mozarts were absent. Wolfgang arrived there after

In his native town Mozart received a monument only 50 years after his death.

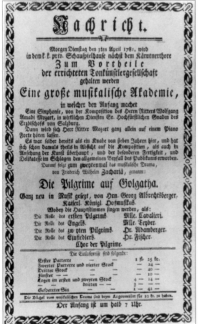

the repeated, specific summons of the Archbishop, only in March of the year 1781. There he was refused permission to give concerts on his own behalf for his Viennese public. He was also obliged to decline all invitations to parties as a private citizen. Concerning this he noted: 'since the Archbishop acts as a great obstacle for me'.

Furthermore, he was made to dine with the cooks and servants - according to the custom of the period. This was just too much for a man of the world, full of success, who had travelled all over Europe. On the first occasion that turned up he broke away.

Because more than once, Mozart wanted to delay his departure, even Colloredo lost his patience. They had a quarrel: 'he advises me to leave this very day, otherwise he is going to write home and have my salary suppressed. There was no way of talking because he burst out like a fire. I listened to it all with great calm - He lied to my face that my salary would be 500 florins - He

Idomeneo, re di Creta. *Frontispiece of the musical compendium for piano of 1796/97.*

In Mozart's days, concerts were announced as 'musical accademies'.

called me a swindler, a rogue, a madman - Oh, I could not write it all down - In the end since my blood was boiling over, I said - So, Your Princely Grace is not satisfied with me? - What, this man wants to threaten me, he's a madman, oh, he's literally mad! - There is the door, look, I will have no more to do with such a swindler - At last I said - Neither do I want anything to do with you - Then he went off - *And I did too*'.

Mozart, consequently, submitted his resignation that was not however accepted. He even failed to respect the summons of the Grand Chamberlain Count Arco. At this point, it was Arco himself who went to fetch the irascible Mozart. Despite his cajoling words, the youth reacted in an implacable manner: 'If he really has such a good opinion of me, then he must try and persuade others with valid arguments - or else leave things as they are - and not use words such as boor and swindler and throw one out of the door with a kick in the behind, but I forget that it was perhaps the Prince's order'.

Contrary, thus, to what is stated in all of his biographies, Mozart was never dismissed in his whole life and it was he who resigned instead; nevertheless his resignations were never officially validated by the Archbishop. From a legal point of view the latter would have been able to force him to return to Salzburg at any time.

Internal courtyard of the Residency palace in Salzburg. In this town, Mozart did not see any possibility of advancement and thus abandoned his post at the Prince-Bishop's.

Concert hall of the palace of the Residence where Mozart and his sister Nannerl also performed.

THE YEARS AS MAESTRO IN VIENNA

The legendary kick of Count Arco suddenly made Mozart become independent and mature. All at once he was able to clearly perceive his need to stand on his own feet. He proudly informed his father Leopold, in his manner, of how Vienna was 'for my trade the best place in the world'.

Mozart expected a wave of novelty from the young Emperor Joseph II, elected just a year earlier. He had always got along with him and counted on his support also for the future, even if he could not expect any help from a financial point of view.

Joseph II referred to the economizing policy that characterized his concept of reform and delegated all the festivities to the nobility and the bourgeoisie, economically very powerful. These were the social settings that after moving to Vienna in 1781, loaded Mozart with so many commissions as to make him write to Salzburg 'after all ... I have, in the end, got tired of keeping up with it all'.

He created almost all his piano concertos in the brief period between 1782 and 1786. Among these are a

Mozart carried out an untiring activity as a mason. His friend, Emanuel Schikaneder also participated in it. Interior views of the 'Zur neugekrönten Höffnung' lodge. Oil painting, 1786 circa.

The old Burgtheater in the Michaelerplatz received from the Emperor Joseph II, in 1776, the new name of 'k.k.National-Hoftheater'. Here the operas Die Entführung aus dem Serail, Le nozze di Figaro and Così fan tutte were performed for the very first time. Water painting by Carl Schütz, 1783 circa.

Mozart's initiation into the masonry was communicated on 5 December 1784 by the 'Zur Wolthätigkeit' lodge to the 'Zur Wahren Eintracht' Bauhütte (lit. building site booth).

In December 1787, Mozart was appointed successor of Christoph Willibald Gluck to the post of k.k.Kammer-Musicus.

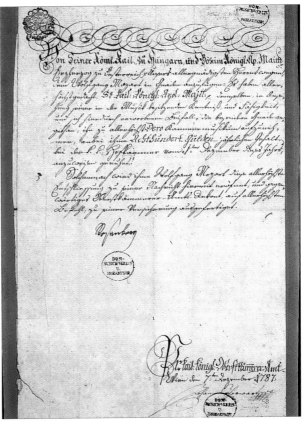

The Fantasia in C Minor (K 475) in Mozart's manuscript.

Canon in four voices 'O du eselhafter Martin' (K 560).

Triumph of the liberal ideas of the Emperor Joseph II. The Emperor is represented in the act of proceeding against corruption and violence and of defending his church reform.

The Peterskirche. Etching by Carl Schütz, 1779. In 1781, Mozart lived on the second floor of the 'Zum Auges Gottes' house (second house to the left) with the Weber family (today Vienna 1, 8 Petersplatz).

few famous works such as the *Concerto in D Minor for Piano* (K 466), that in *E Flat Major* (K 482), the Concerto in *A Major for Piano* (K 488) or that in *D Major* (K 503). Also symphonies date back to those years spent in Vienna such as the *Symphony in D Major ("Symphony of Prague")* (K 504), the *Symphony in E Flat Major* (K 543), the *Symphony in G Minor* (K 550) or *the Jupiter Symphony in C Major* (K 551). Naturally one must not forget the Lieder *Das Veilchen (The Violet)* (K 476), *Abendempfindung (Evening Sensations)* (K 523), *An Chloë (To Cloe)* (K 524) or *Sehnsucht nach dem Frühling (Komm Lieber Mai) (Nostalgia of Spring, Come Dear May)* (K 596). In those years, he also wrote numerous piano compositions for almost daily performances. The Viennese aristocracy was extremely

The magnificent pulpit of the
Peterskirche is the work of M. Steindl.

According to legend, the Peterskirche was founded by Charlemagne. Its
current Baroque style largely dates back to the work of Lukas von
Hildenbrandt (1668-1745).

interested in Mozart's talent. He also wrote arias which include that dedicated to Aloysia Weber whom, after his unrequited love in Mannheim, he met again as a married woman, in Vienna. He even lived, for a brief period, with the Weber family in their bourgeoisie residence *Zum Auge Gottes*. This time, though, the object of his attention was different, the love of his life became Aloysia's sister, Constanze. She was the "kindest and the cleverest" of the Weber sisters. Their marriage took place on 4 August, 1782 in St Stephen's Cathedral. Only two of Mozart's six children survived: Carl Thomas (1784-1858) and Franz Xaver (1791-1844), while Constanze outlived her husband by 51 years reaching the age of ninety.

Pages 38-39:

Constanze Mozart, portrayed in 1782 by her brother-in-law Joseph Lange, actor and painter.

St Stephen's Cathedral testified the crucial events of the Mozart family: the children were baptized here, the confessor for Mozart's last rites was from here, and here Mozart was blessed.

The Opera of the Viennese state was strictly connected to the operas of Mozart since its inauguration in 1869 when Don Giovanni *was staged.*

THE VIENNESE SINGSPIEL AND THE NEW HEIGHTS OF OPERA

The Viennese years were for Mozart a stimulus for fine creations not only in the field of concert music. He developed an unfailing dramatic instinct also as a composer of operas. He proved to be an innovator also in the Singspiel *Die Entführung aus dem Serail (The Rape from the Seraglio)* (K 384), based on a text by Gottlieb Stephanie the younger. At the time, singing in German was not at all common. On the contrary, anything that came from Italy - the land of song - was more highly appreciated and better remunerated.

Along the Graben. Copper-plate engraving by Carl
Schütz, 1782. In 1781/82 Mozart lived in the house
at 17 Graben and, in 1784, with Constanze,
at no. 29 (Trattnerhof).

Pierre-Augustin Caron de Beaumarchais (1732-1799),
the creator of the figure Figaro, that later became a
prototype. Copper-plate engraving by an anonymous
artist.

The Emperor Leopold I had the Pestsaüle (column to the
plague) erected following a vow made during the great
plague of 1679.

To prove how even Austria was able to create its own tradition, the Emperor Joseph II inaugurated the royal imperial court Nationaltheater that, from then, began staging for years to come, German-language operas.

The most applauded of these remained, nevertheless, together with *Der Schauspieldirektor (the Impresario)* (K 486), *Die Entführung aus dem Serail.*

By chance, the female protagonist was called Constanze, as Mozart's fiancée whom he was to marry a month after the inauguration of this opera.

Indications of Mozart's happy marriage are to be found, even three years and a half later, in *Le nozze di Figaro* (K 492) in which he gave to the figure of Susanna several of Constanze's undeniable traits. With the help of the Countess, she manages to completely confound both the

Gottlieb Stephanie the younger composed the libretto for Die Entführung aus dem Serail. *The etching is presumably the work of the Tirolese miniaturist Joseph A. Kappeller (1761 - 1806).*

Scenes from 'La Folle Journée ou Le Mariage de Figaro' by Beaumarchais. Illustration in the libretto published in 1785.

The German translation of the plays by Beaumarchais, printed in 1785.

Neues Singspiel.

Im kaiserl. königl. National-Hof-Theater
wird heute Montag den 1ten May 1786 aufgeführt:
(zum erstenmal)

LE NOZZE
DI FIGARO.

Die Hochzeit des Figaro.

Ein italiänisches Singspiel in vier Aufzügen.
Die Musik ist vom Herrn Kapellmeister Mozart.

Die Bücher sind italiänisch und deutsch jedes für 20 kr. beym Logenmeister zu haben.

Der Anfang ist um halb 7 Uhr.

The theatrical programme of the first performance in the k.k.National-Hoftheater of Vienna, 1786.

Mozart's musical draft for a duette of the Nozze di Figaro.

unfaithful Count, who tries to seduce her, and her jealous fiancé, Figaro. The theme of this opera is based on the famous comedy *La Folle Journée ou Le Mariage de Figaro* written in Paris between 1778 and 1784 by Pierre Augustin Caron de Beaumarchais. Already the year before, Mozart and the versifier of the text, Lorenzo Da Ponte, had set to work to adapt the subject of the *jus primae noctis,* then of great interest, for use in an opera libretto of great effect. Intrigues and jealousies are introduced even in the genesis of this amusing opera that Mozart composed, this time too, in Italian. Due to its burning political content, the

43

comedy had already caused disorders in France. In Vienna it had been banned by censorship because of it featured social criticism. However, an exception was made for Mozart who had managed to convince the Emperor Joseph that his adaptation in opera form was inoffensive. The first performance took place on 1 March, 1786 in the royal imperial court Nationaltheater, meeting initially with little success but, in the end, obtaining one of the greatest ever enjoyed by Mozart. During their collaboration, Mozart and Da Ponte had got on very well together. The Italian Abbé Da Ponte, originally of Jewish faith and later a Christian convert, and the Salzburg Wolfgang Amadeus Mozart, who moved to Vienna in the same period, shared the same joy of living. They decided to continue to work together and, with *Don Giovanni* (K 527) (1787) and *Così fan tutte* (K 588) (1790), reached new, lofty heights.

Lorenzo Da Ponte (1749-1838) was a librettist and a friend of Mozart's.

VIENNESE SOCIETY AND IDYLLIC FAMILY LIFE

Mozart had probably first met Lorenzo Da Ponte in an evening among friends. Maybe at the Herberstein's, the Mesmer's - when Mozart was twelve years old he had performed *Bastien und Bastienne* (K 46b/50) in the garden of their home at 29 Rasumofskygasse, in the third district - or in the home of Jewish families, the Arnsteins or Plankensteins, a member of which, the Baron Wetzlar von Plankenstein, a dear friend of Mozart's and godfather of his firstborn Raimund, was the landlord of his house at 7 Kohlmarkt, in the first district where the composer lived in 1783. Instead, he composed *Figaro* in one of the noblest establishments in Vienna: 8 Schulerstrasse / 5 Domgasse in the first district. This house, that is still standing, has been transformed into a museum and has taken on a new appearance through the restoration works of 1995 (opening time: from Tues. to Sun. from 10 A.M. to 6 P.M.).

In 1781 Mozart live in the Arnstein home, in which Fanny graced one of the famous salons of the period.

The blind musician Maria Theresia von Paradis was one of Mozart's most talented pupils.

'Der Schnepfen - Strich' (lit. the passage of the woodcocks). This was how the passage of the prostitutes along the Graben of Vienna was called. Coloured copper-plate engraving by Johann Hieronymus Löschenkohl, 1780 circa.

Antonio Salieri. Oil painting by Joseph Willibrord Mähler (1778-1860). According to the legend fueled by the 'Amadeus Kult', he poisoned Mozart; strong suspicions, confuted however by scientific tests and by documents of the period. His post as Hofkapellmeister in Vienna was already more than assured for Salieri, while Mozart didn't stand any real chance of obtaining it.

Mozart's daily life in Vienna followed a rigid timetable: 'by 6 in the morning my hair is already dressed. - By 7 I am fully dressed. - I then write till 9 o'clock. From 9 to 1 o'clock I give lessons. - I then dine unless I am invited out, in which case we dine at 2 or even at past 3 o'clock, as today and tomorrow at the Countess Zizi's and Countess Thun's. - I cannot work before 5 or 6 - and often I am prevented by a concert; otherwise I write till 9. - Then I go to see my dear Constanze …at half past 11 or at 11 I get home; …especially if I get home somewhat early, I am accustomed to writing something before going to bed. - In this case I often write on till 1 o'clock. - and I am up again at 6'. Mozart earned huge sums in this period. He performed in the so-called subscription concerts, he accepted commissions for compositions, obtained commissions for operas and followed his pupils. After all, they too must have had an extraordinary talent. One of them was the blind composer and pianist Teresa Paradis of whom there remain, still today, excellent compositions. We must also mention Countess Caroline Lumbeke, Countess Waldstätten, Countess Palffy, as well as the professional pianist Josepha von Auernhammer who nurtured deep affection for her maestro and wanted to marry him at all costs. Mozart, on the contrary, was not in the least in love with her and clearly declared on his part: 'the lady is a scarecrow!' Well, a gentleman doesn't use this sort of language! And Mozart always wanted to be considered as such.

He behaved more gallantly with the eighteen-year-old Maria Teresa Trattner, wife of the opulent fifty-nine-year-old editor, Johann Thomas von Trattner. As a married man, Mozart even went to live in one of the bourgeois homes of the family, in the 'Trattnerhof' (29/29A Graben, in the first district).

Mozart was considered, since the beginning, to be among the most important personalities of Vienna.

The 'Figaro Haus' in Vienna, 5 Domgasse (quarter 1), in which Mozart lived from 1784 to 1787. Here he composed Le Nozze di Figaro.

Stuccoed ceiling of Mozart's supposed studio in the 'Figaro Haus', the most famous commemorative site of Mozart in Vienna.

HIS LAST YEARS

Even in Vienna, however, Mozart's professional life didn't manage to consolidate itself in a completely satisfactory way. When it came to offering a post, he was always put off. Still today we do not know the reason why. It was probably due to the unconventional ways of Mozart together with his occasional villainy. Naturally no civil servant of the imperial administration wanted to have anything to do with him and thus the conservative nobility (in contrast with the liberal Joseph II) tried to prevent, for as long as possible, access to the position to such an intrusive person. Finally, in December, 1787, he was appointed *k.k.Kammer-Musicus* in the Court chamber orchestra succeeding the deceased Christoph Willibald Gluck. His salary was certainly lower than that of his predecessor, but Mozart was also a good deal younger.

The participation of Austria, a Russian ally, in the war against the Turks (1788) caused a significant economic recession. The court and

Copy of the original of the Kleine Nachtmusik *(K 384a/388), of the year 1782.*

In the Civic Repertory Theatre of Prague, Mozart made known his Figaro. *Here also* Don Giovanni *and* Titus *were performed for the first time. Coloured copper-plate engraving by Caspar Pluth, 1796.*

Coronation of Leopold II as Emperor, on 9 October 1790, in which also Mozart participated. The anonymous copperplate engraving shows the procession from the Cathedral to the Römer, the town house of Frankfurt.

Entrance of Leopold II to Frankfurt for his coronation as Emperor. Copper-plate engraving.

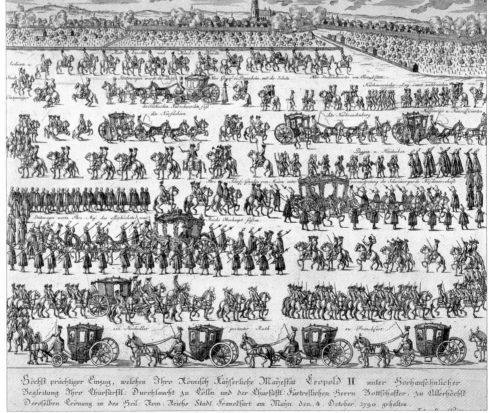

Table companions of the Emperor Leopold II. Oil painting by Maria Catharina Gürtler, 1792.

The Emperor Joseph II with his brother, the Granduke Leopold of Tuscany. Painting by Pompeo Batoni, 1769. His mother Maria Teresa had, on her part, advised the Granduke not to take Mozart into his service.

the nobility were no longer as prodigal as the year before. The population rose up to protest against the tax increases and artists immediately felt the repercussions of the crisis. Now, managing to obtain commissions implied an even more arduous fight. Many had to limit their needs. Mozart, on the other hand, maintained his high lifestyle, played for money in society, and allowed himself expensive houses. However, the recession did not improve. Despite Mozart's auspices, his load of debts did not lessen. He tried to pay them off with new loans. His difficult situation is documented by numerous petitions written to his lodge brother, Michael Puchberg (Mozart had be-

come a mason in 1784). Mozart himself spoke of his 'collapse - which was certainly not my fault'. With these words, he could not but be referring to his erroneous judgement of the economic situation of Austria. Nevertheless, in 1787, Mozart dedicated himself constantly and with unerring hope, to his compositions. His collaboration with Da Ponte had further consolidated itself. He had received, for the civic repertory theatre of Prague, a commission for *Don Giovanni* (K 527), a story used by others several times before for comedies and operas. Mozart's second trip to Prague is associated with the first performance of this opera. This performance was held on the

occasion of the inauguration of *Figaro,* that had made him particularly happy. In Prague, he was received each time with great enthusiasm ('I would have liked my good friends to be here even only for one evening to take part in my joy!'). The entire society in which he lived, his private life, and his new Masonic ideals produced in this period a profound transformation in his outlook. Many of his new convictions were transposed in his immediate and highly expressive style of composition, so that he seemed suddenly to look ahead to the future century.
In *Don Giovanni* he projects himself musically, in part already into the Romantic Age (thus Mozart's opera

La Clemenza di Tito
Opera seria
Del Sign. W. A. Mozart
Aggiustata per il Piano Forte
Del Sign. A. E. Müller

In Hamburgo presso Günther e Böhme

Die Zauberflöte.

Eine

große Oper in zwey Aufzügen.

Von

Emmanuel Schikaneder.

Die Musik ist von Herrn Wolfgang Amade
Mozart, Kapellmeister, und wirklichem k.
k. Kammer-Compositeur.

*Compendium of music for piano of the
Clemenza di Tito (K 621). Frontispiece
of the first edition.*

*Libretto of Emanuel Schikaneder for
the opera the Zauberflöte.*

was truly the most highly appreciated by romanticism). Elsewhere, for example in the finale of the minuette of the *Symphony in G Minor* (K 550), he heralds atonality, a method of composition that was to receive a theoretical definition only in the twentieth century. One of the most popular compositions of Mozart's

The fountain of Papageno in Salzburg.

*Emanuel Schikaneder as Papageno.
Engraving by Ignaz Alberti, 1791.*

last years of life was the *Serenata in
G Major (Eine kleine Nachtmusik)
(A Little Seranade)* (1787); this title,
like many others, was not chosen by
Mozart!

Two years later, Mozart went on a
two month trip to Berlin, at the invi-
tation of the Prince Karl Lichnowsky
with intermediary stops in Prague

Es lebe SARASTRO.
Achzehenter Auftritt I Act.

Sarastro's stage entrance. Coloured copper-plate engraving of the brothers Joseph and Peter Schaffer, 1793 circa.

Picture of a scene of the Zauberflöte from a performance in the Felsenreitschule (school of rock horseriding) of Salzburg.

and Dresda. The journey, free of charge for Mozart (Lichnowsky, a mason friend who was also on a business trip, shouldered the musician's expenses), earned him numerous commissions: six *String Quartets* and six *Easy Sonatas for Piano* for the Princess Friederike Charlotte.

The première of the opera *Così fan tutte* (K 588), revolving around the theme of the multiple forms of love and faithfulness and based on a real Viennese event, took place in 1790. The situation concerning commissions - in direct relation with Mozart's fame - was not bad. In this period there was only a reduction in the number of pupils who could afford high fees and in the orders for occasional compositions.

In February 1790, Joseph II died. To earn the favour of Leopold II, in the meantime elected Emperor of Austria, Mozart participated in the Autumn of the same year in Frankfurt, in his coronation, also visiting Mainz, Mannheim, Augsburg, and Monaco. He consequently received a commission for *La clemenza di Tito* (K 621) to celebrate the coronation in Prague (his third visit to this city). He also unexpectedly received the request of the mysterious messenger, Franz Anton Leitgeb, for the *Requiem* (K 626) that the amateur composer, Count Walsegg-Stuppach ordered for his deceased wife and that he was to later pass off as his own. In the same period, a month and a half before his death, Mozart dedicated himself to the transcription of the fairy opera *Die Zauberflöte (The Magic Flute)* (K 620) according to the favourite popular Viennese Baroque style, with numerous elements of the opera seria. The first performance was held on 30 September, 1791, in the 'Freihaustheater auf dem Wieden' that was at 25 Operngasse, in the first district. The role of

Portrait of the 'sombre messenger' - so defined by Grillparzer - Franz Anton Leitgeb, who delivered to Mozart the commission for the Requiem. *Painting of 1797 circa.*

The Theresienbad in Baden near Vienna. This small town was the favourite seaside resort of the Viennese. Mozart went there several times to visit his wife. Coloured copper-plate engraving by Johann Ziegler.

Pages 56-57:

Portrait of W. A. Mozart, engraving by Johann Neidl from a painting by Posch.

Constanze Mozart, anonymous pastel portrait. Constanze outlives Mozart by 51 years.

Posch fec. Joh. Neidl. sc.

W. A. Mozart

Papageno was played by the impresario of the theatre and librettist of *Die Zauberflöte*, Emanuel Schikaneder.

Mozart composed intensely and, in the meantime, continually complained of the absence of the wife Constanze who, seriously ill, had to undergo weekly treatments in Baden, near Vienna.

Suffering from nervous rheumatic fever ('a violent miliary fever'), Wolfgang Amadeus Mozart died suddenly on the morning of 5 December, 1791, five minutes before 1 o'clock. A crowd of female and male admirers, mourning the death of the musician, gathered under his window at 5 Rauhensteingasse, in the first district.

Constanze was so grief stricken that she laid down beside the corpse hoping to be infected, her too, by the disease.

St Stephen's Cathedral seen from the north, with the Chapel of the Cross, whose entrance is visible on the right near the pulpit of Capistrano. Coloured copper-plate engraving by Carl Schütz.

The interior of St Stephen's Cathedral. Engraving by Melchior Seltsam, 1816. In September 1791, Mozart was also nominated Vice-Kapellmeister to the Cathedral (unpaid).

The oldest surviving view of St Stephen's Cathedral. Mozart was blessed at 3 P.M., in the Chapel of the Cross.

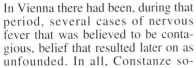

which caused her to suffer from leg sores consequent to the repeated inflammation of the veins. At the death of her husband she had to, for the first time, depend solely on herself, and face, together with moral distress, serious financial difficulties. Mozart had not thought of protecting his family with a social insurance which was, even then, a totally uncommon practice among artists. Constanze was thus obliged to sell

The house where Mozart died, Vienna 1, 8 Rauhensteingasse. Watercoloured pen drawing by Emil Hütter, 1806.

The parsimonious Josephine tomb, whose base could be opened and therefore used more than once.

Mozart's death certificate. Vienna, December 1791.

In Vienna there had been, during that period, several cases of nervous fever that was believed to be contagious, belief that resulted later on as unfounded. In all, Constanze sojourned four times in Baden for treatments. She had gone through five childbirths up till then (moreover, not long before, she had become pregnant with Franz Xaver)

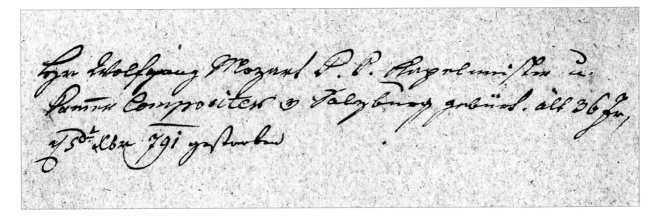

most of their furniture and musical material to cancel, first of all, Mozart's debts. In this, she proved to be an able businesswoman. Dominated by Mozart, the family head, affectionate but despotic, who personally saw to his children's daily nutrition, she had never been able to develop her talent.

In 1809, Constanze married again, to be precise with a great admirer of Mozart's the legation counsellor, Georg Nikolaus von Nissen, author together with Constanze of the first extensive biography of the musician, submitted for publication by his wife in 1828, two years after his death. The reasons for which she went to search for Mozart's tomb in the St

The legation counsellor Georg Nikolaus Nissen, Constanze's second husband. Oil painting by Ferdinand Jagemann, 1809.

The so-called Catalogo-Köchel includes all the works by Mozart. It was published for the first time in Lipsia in 1862.

Marxer Friedhof (Cemetery of St Mark) only eighteen years after his death, has never been explained.

The circumstances of Mozart's funeral have been accurately investigated in the past years. The question asked has always been the same: Why did no-one attend his funeral?

The Josephine Orders concerning funerals, do not envisage in the least that relatives accompany their dead to the cemetery. In Mozart's case, the St Marxer Friedhof was a good four and a half kilometres away from

the Chapel of the Cross in St Stephen's. Reaching it would have represented a certain undertaking even for the fittest. The corpse, lifted onto a carriage pulled by horses, was escorted only by the sexton up to the cemetery and here it was sometimes, according to the weather conditions, only placed in the coffin, to be then buried a few days later.

Mozart at least had a coffin all to himself. According to the register of St Stephen's Cathedral, the blessing took place on 6 December, while the

The Mozart family tomb in Sebastians-Friedhof in Salzburg.

Present-day funeral monument of W. A. Mozart in the St Marxer Friedhof in Vienna.

The monument to Mozart in the Burggarten in Vienna, by Viktor Tilgner, of the year 1896.

Mozart's tomb in the St Marxer Friedhof in Salzburg. Historical photograph of 1891.

funeral itself was to be carried out on 7 December, 1791. According to the information that has come down to us, the bad weather coincides only with this day.

This is certainly not the only part of Mozart's life which we must draw light on. He remains one of the unsolved enigmas in the history of our culture.

BIOGRAPHY

1756 27 January: birth of Wolfgang (Amadeus) Mozart. He is one of the two surviving children, including Nannerl, and the youngest child of the violin-master, Leopold Mozart, a native of Augusta, instrumentalist to the Court Chapel of Salzburg, and of his wife Anna Maria, a native of St Gilgen in Salzkammergut.

1760 The first signs of the exceptional musical talents of Wolfgang.

1761 The first compositions and the first public performance.

1762 The family's journey to Munich and to Vienna for concerts. Performance at the Court of Maria Teresa.

1763 Beginning of the grand tour through almost all the important towns in Germany up to Brussels, Paris and Versailles.

1764 Continuation of the journey to London. Performance at the English Royal Court. Mozart creates his first symphonies.

1765 Sojourn in Belgium and Holland.

1766 Return trip to Salzburg through France and Switzerland.

1769 Mozart's appointment as third Konzertmeister to the Court Chapel of Salzburg (unpaid). Beginning of his first journey to Italy.

1770 Sojourns for study in Verona, Milan, Bologna, Florence, Rome, and Naples. First performance of *Mitridate, re di Ponto*.

1771 Second journey to Italy.

1772 Mozart becomes *Konzertmeister* (paid) of the new Prince Hieronymus Colloredo. Third trip to Italy. Last performance in this country of one of his operas: *Lucio Silla*.

1777 Dismissal of the Mozarts, father and son, from the Court Chapel of Salzburg by Hieronymus Colleredo. A month later, Leopold is taken on again. Beginning of the grand tour of Mozart and his mother, Anna Maria, of Germany and to Paris.

1778 Friendship with the Weber family in Mannheim. Continuation of the trip to Paris. Death of Mozart's mother. Return to Salzburg.

1779 Readmission to the Salzburg service as Court-organist.

1781 First performance of *Idomeneo, re di Creta* in Munich. Departure for Vienna on strict order of the Archbishop. Conflicts with the entire Court of Salzburg. Definitive break with Colloredo. Mozart abandons, in dramatic circumstances, his post at the Court of Salzburg. From this time on he lived in Vienna.

1782 First performance of *Die Entführung aus dem Serail*. Marriage to Constanze Weber.

1783 Last visit of Mozart to Salzburg. Birth of his first child, Raimund Leopold - who dies two months later.

1784 Mozart's initiation into the Masonic lodge 'Zur Wohlthätigkeit'. Nannerl marries Johann Baptist von Berchtold zu Sonnenburg. Birth of Mozart's child Carl Thomas - who lived up to the age of 74.

1786 First performance of the opera *Der Schauspieldirektor* and, a few months later, of *Le nozze di Figaro*. Birth of Mozart's third child, Thomas Leopold - who dies shortly after.

1787 Mozart's first journey to Prague where he directs his *Figaro*. Death of Leopold Mozart in Salzburg. Second journey to Prague and first performance of *Don Giovanni*. Return to Vienna, where in December the musician is appointed 'k.k.Kammer-Musicus'. He creates *Kleine Nachtmusik*. Birth of his third child, Teresa - she too dies, five months later.

1788 Mozart composes his last three symphonies: in *E Flat Major*, in *G Minor* and the *Jupiter Symphony in C Major*.

1789 Journey to Berlin through Dresda and Lipsia. Constanze's first therapeutic stay in Baden. Birth of their fifth child, Anna Maria - dies.

1790 First performance of *Così fan tutte*. Constanze is once again under treatment in Baden. Departure of Mozart for Frankfurt for Emperor Leopold II's coronation.

1791 Mozart obtains, after prolonged uncertainty a post as *Vice-Kapellmeister* (unpaid) to St Stephen's Cathedral. Another sojourn of Constanze for treatment in Baden. Birth of their sixth child Franz Xaver Wolfgang who lived up to the age of 53. Third journey to Prague. First performance in this town of the opera for the coronation, *La clemenza di Tito*. Beginning of the transcription of *Requiem* (it remains unfinished). First performance of *Zauberflöte*. Mozart falls ill. He dies on 5 December at one o'clock in the morning.

BIBLIOGRAPHY OF MOZART

Abert, Hermann: Wolfgang Amadeus Mozart. Zwei Bände und Register. Wien 1983.

Becker, Max (Hg.): Mozart. Sein Leben und seine Zeit in Texten und Bildern. Frankfurt 1991.

Braunbehrens, Volkmar: Mozart in Wien. München 1991.

Deutsch, Otto Erich / Eibl, Joseph Heinz (Hg.): Mozart. Dokumente seines Lebens (Auswahl). Kassel 1981. Paperback edition: dtv Dok 2927, München 1991.

Einstein, Alfred: Mozart. Sein Charakter – sein Werk. Frankfurt 1985. Paperback edition: Fischer TB 2039, Frankfurt 1991.

Gruber, Gernot: Mozart. Leben und Werk in Texten und Bildern. Insel TB 1695, Frankfurt 1995.

Hildesheimer, Wolfgang: Mozart. Biographie. Frankfurt 1990. Paperback edition: Suhrkamp TB 598, Frankfurt 1992.

Kunze, Stefan: Mozarts Opern. Stuttgart 1984.

Landon, Howard C. Robbins: 1791. Mozarts letztes Jahr. Kassel 1992. Paperback edition: dtv Sachb. 30033, München 1992.

Nagel, Ivan: Autonomie und Gnade. Über Mozarts Opern. München 1988.

Niemetschek, Franz Xaver: Ich kannte Mozart. Leben des K. K. Kapellmeisters W. A. Mozart, nach Originalquellen beschrieben. München 1991.

Publig, Maria: Mozart. Ein unbeirrbares Leben. München 1991.

Tschitscherin, Georgi W.: Mozart. Eine Studie. rororo Sachb. 8389, Hamburg 1987.